LET'S LEARN
FRENCH

Written and edited by
Nicola Wright, Carol Watson and Philippa Moyle

Illustrated by
Kim Woolley and Teresa Foster

COURAGE
B O O K S
An imprint of
Running Press
Philadelphia • London

Contents

This book was created by
Zigzag Publishing Ltd, The Barn,
Randolph's Farm, Brighton Road,
Hurstpierpoint, BN6 9EL, England

Designers: Teresa Foster, Jane Felstead,
 Suzi Hooper, Jenny Searle and
 Jonathan Skelton
Design Manager: Kate Buxton
Additional illustrations: Guy Smith
Consultants: Claire Nozières and
 Katherine Folliot
Pronunciation guide: Philippa Tomlinson
 and Kay Barnham
Series concept: Tony Potter

8319
Color separations by RCS Graphics Ltd, Leeds

9 8 7 6 5 4 3 2 1
Digit on the right indicates the number of this printing.

ISBN 1-56138-738-X

This book may be ordered by mail from the publisher.
But try your bookstore first!
Published by Courage Books, and imprint of
Running Press Book Publishers
125 South Twenty-second Street
Philadelphia, Pennsylvania 19103-4399

About this book

In this book you can find out all about France, French people and the French language. Discover what the French like to eat and drink, what they do for a living and what famous French places look like.

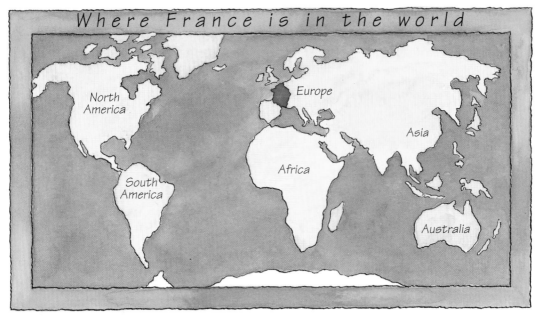

Where France is in the world

North America

South America

Europe

Africa

Asia

Australia

Find out what French children do in their spare time and how they celebrate French festivals.

From page 26 onwards, you can learn how to speak French.

Hello!

Bonjour!

You will meet the Flaubert family and see what they say in lots of situations. They show you how to say the French words. You will find many useful French words and phrases throughout this book to help you increase your French vocabulary.

Map of France

France is one of the largest countries in Europe. It is bordered by seven other countries: Belgium, Luxembourg, Germany, Switzerland, Italy, Andorra, and Spain. Even so, almost half of France's border is coastline.

Longest river:
The Loire, 634 miles (1,020 km). Many beautiful **châteaux** line its banks.

le fleuve
river

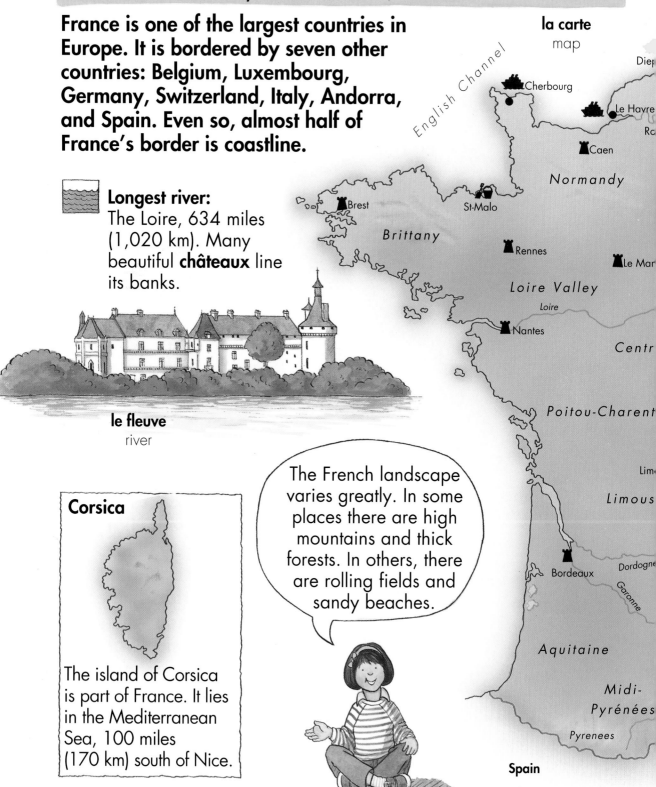

la carte
map

English Channel

Diep

Cherbourg

Le Havre

Ro

Caen

Normandy

Brest

St-Malo

Brittany

Rennes

Le Mar

Loire Valley

Loire

Nantes

Centr

Poitou-Charent

Lim

Limous

Bordeaux

Dordogne

Garonne

Aquitaine

Midi-Pyrénées

Pyrenees

Spain

The French landscape varies greatly. In some places there are high mountains and thick forests. In others, there are rolling fields and sandy beaches.

Corsica

The island of Corsica is part of France. It lies in the Mediterranean Sea, 100 miles (170 km) south of Nice.

4

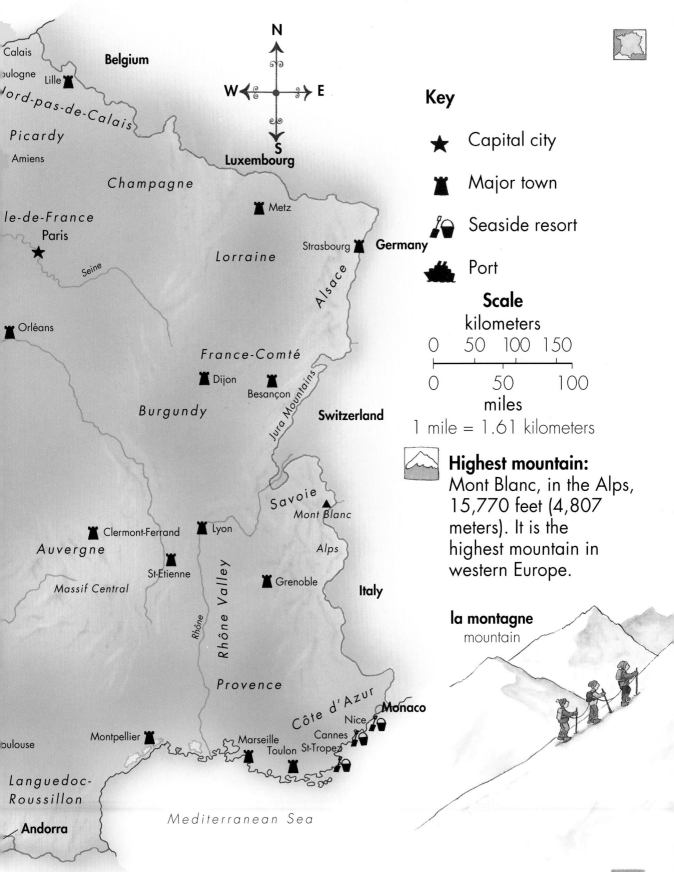

Calais

Boulogne

Lille

Belgium

Nord-pas-de-Calais

Picardy

Amiens

Champagne

N

W ← → **E**

S

Luxembourg

Metz

Key

★ Capital city

♜ Major town

🪣 Seaside resort

🚢 Port

Ile-de-France

★ Paris

Seine

Lorraine

Strasbourg

Germany

Alsace

Orléans

France-Comté

Dijon

Besançon

Jura Mountains

Switzerland

Burgundy

Savoie

▲ Mont Blanc

Clermont-Ferrand

Lyon

Auvergne

Alps

St-Etienne

Grenoble

Italy

Massif Central

Rhône Valley

Rhône

Provence

Montpellier

Côte d'Azur

Monaco

Nice

Cannes

Toulouse

Marseille

Toulon

St-Tropez

Languedoc-Roussillon

Andorra

Mediterranean Sea

Scale

kilometers

0   50   100   150

0   50   100

miles

1 mile = 1.61 kilometers

Highest mountain:
Mont Blanc, in the Alps,
15,770 feet (4,807
meters). It is the
highest mountain in
western Europe.

la montagne
mountain

5

Facts about France

Although France is about the size of Texas, almost three times as many people live there, so it is much more crowded.

Size: 220,668 sq miles (543,965 sq km)

Population: 56,555,700

This has been the French flag since the French Revolution in 1789. It is called the **tricolore** which means a flag with three stripes.

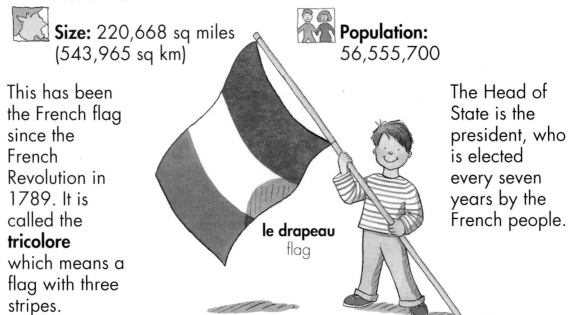

le drapeau
flag

The Head of State is the president, who is elected every seven years by the French people.

Language

Although the official language is French, there are other languages spoken in parts of the country:

la langue
language

Breton is spoken in the northwest. It is related to Cornish, Welsh, and Irish.

Basque is spoken in the region around the Spanish border. It is unlike any other European language.

German is spoken in Alsace and Lorraine, as these regions once belonged to Germany.

Money

French money is divided into **francs** (F) and **centimes** (ct). 100 centimes equals 1 franc.

l'argent
money

Bank notes are issued for the following amounts: 500, 200, 100, 50, and 20 francs. The heads of famous French people appear on the notes.

There are 10, 5, 2, 1, and ½ franc coins, and 20, 10, and 5 centime coins. The woman shown on the back of the coins is **Liberté**, representing freedom.

la pièce de monnaie
coin

le billet de banque
banknote

Capital city:
Paris

Official name:
La République Française
(French Republic)

Some things France is well known for

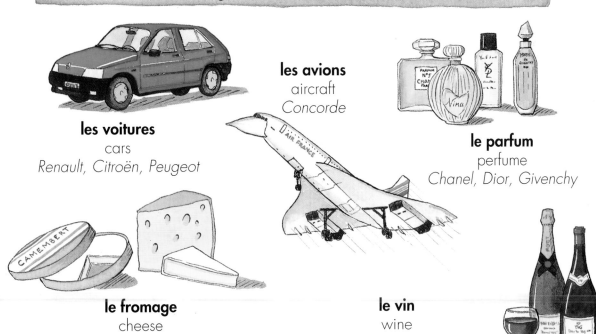

les avions
aircraft
Concorde

les voitures
cars
Renault, Citroën, Peugeot

le parfum
perfume
Chanel, Dior, Givenchy

le fromage
cheese
Cambert, Brie, Roquefort

le vin
wine
Bordeaux, Champagne, Burgundy

Regions of France

France is divided into many different regions, and includes the island of Corsica in the Mediterranean. The scenery, weather, and way of life vary greatly from region to region.

The north of France has cold winters, warm summers, and plenty of rainfall.

le temps
weather

le nord
north

le sud
south

In the south of France it is hot and dry in the summer and warm and sunny in the winter.

Many of the seaside resorts along the south coast, such as Cannes and Nice, were once small fishing ports. Now they are vacation places for people from all over Europe.

The French call the south coast the **Côte d'Azur**, which means "sky-blue coast," because of its good weather

le ski nautique
waterskiing

About one fifth of France is covered with forests. The Vosges and Jura mountains in the east are covered with pine and fir trees.

la forêt
forest

Wild animals, including boar, foxes, beavers, and chamois (a kind of antelope) can be found in these regions.

In the east, the high mountains of the Alps are covered with snow all year and the scenery is spectacular.

faire du ski
skiing

This region is very popular for skiing in the winter and hiking in summer.

la neige
snow

Normandy, in the north, has a flat coastline with long sandy beaches.

la côte
coast

The coastline of Brittany in the northwest is rocky with many inlets.

la plage
beach

Several large rivers run through the high, flat land of central France. Beautiful countryside and picturesque towns line their banks.

There are vineyards all over France. Most regions produce their own wine. Champagne and Burgundy are some of the best known.

le raisin
grape

le vignoble
vineyard

9

Paris

Paris is the largest and most important French city. It is the capital of the country and the center of industry, business, fashion, and entertainment.

The original city was built on an island in the middle of the River Seine. The island became known as the **Ile de la Cité** (City Island). During the twelfth century, the beautiful Notre-Dame cathedral was built on it.

Notre-Dame Cathedral

l'artiste
artist

Paris is famous for its arts. There are many street painters in the district called Montmartre. Famous artists like Renoir and Picasso once lived there.

The quickest and cheapest way to get around the city is on **le Métro** (the subway).

Over 10,200,000 people live in Paris and its suburbs, which is almost one fifth of the total French population.

les gens
people

RATP

Palais du Louvre and the glass pyramids (art museum)

Sacré-Cœur
(church on top of the hill of Montmartre with splendid views of Paris)

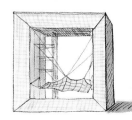

Arche de la Défense
(built to mark 200 years since the French Revolution)

Arc de Triomphe
(the Tomb of the Unknown Soldier is under it)

Eiffel Tower
(built in 1889 for an exhibition)

Panthéon
(church containing the tombs of some of those people who died during the Revolution)

Place de la Concorde
(many people were guillotined here during the Revolution)

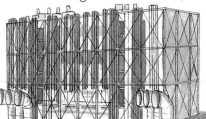

Pompidou Center
(modern exhibition halls)

Moulin Rouge
(one of the most famous nightclubs in Paris)

In a typical French town

There is a square in the middle of most French towns and villages. All the main shops are grouped around it. Often there is a statue or water fountain in the center.

la boulangerie
bakery

le magasin
shop

People gather to talk in the main square under the shade of trees.

la charcuterie
delicatessen

le supermarché
supermarket

Les agents de police patrol in the towns. **Les gendarmes** patrol the countryside. Both types of police wear a blue uniform.

la poste
post office

l'épicerie
grocery store

la librairie-papeterie-maison de la presse
bookstore-stationers-newspaper shop

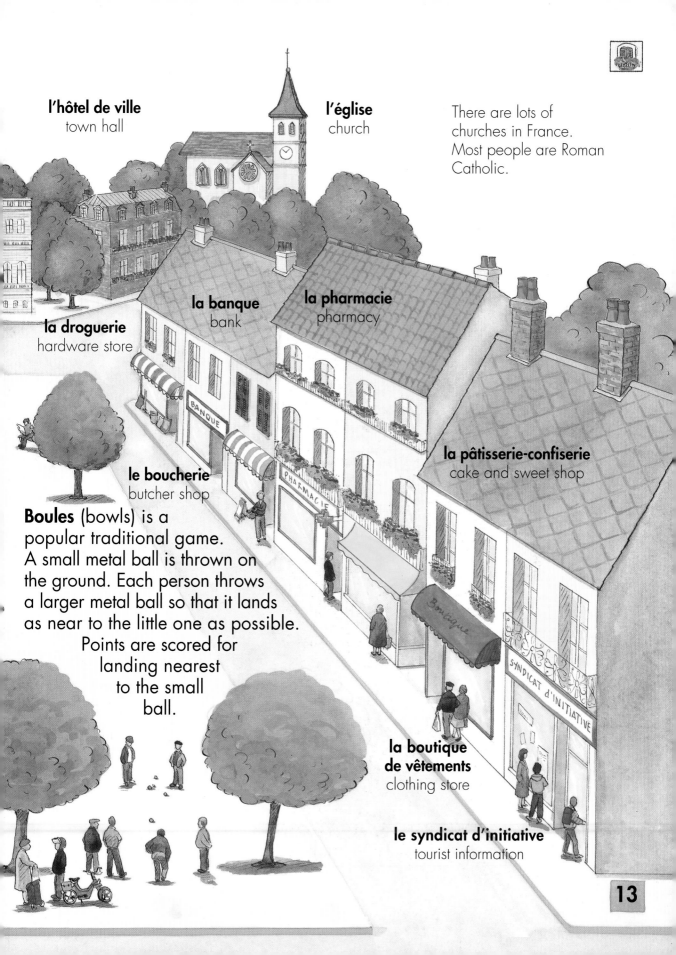

l'hôtel de ville
town hall

l'église
church

There are lots of churches in France. Most people are Roman Catholic.

la droguerie
hardware store

la banque
bank

la pharmacie
pharmacy

le boucherie
butcher shop

la pâtisserie-confiserie
cake and sweet shop

Boules (bowls) is a popular traditional game. A small metal ball is thrown on the ground. Each person throws a larger metal ball so that it lands as near to the little one as possible. Points are scored for landing nearest to the small ball.

la boutique de vêtements
clothing store

le syndicat d'initiative
tourist information

13

Eating in France

The French are famous for their love of food and cooking. Meals are never rushed and French restaurants are some of the best in the world.

Here is a typical French breakfast **(le petit déjeuner)** called a continental breakfast:

la confiture
jam

le beurre
butter

la baguette
long French loaf

le croissant
flaky, crescent-shaped roll

le café
coffee

le chocalat chaud
hot chocolate

We drink our chocolate from bowls, and we like to dip bread into it.

Here are some typical French dishes:

le bœuf bourguignon
a beef stew cooked in red wine

la quiche lorraine
bacon and egg custard

la salade niçoise

olives, anchovies, tomatoes, onions, and tuna fish

les crêpes
pancakes

la tarte Tatin
apple and custard pie

le pâté
pâté

les escargots
snails

les moules
mussels

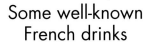

Some well-known French drinks

l'apéritif
before-dinner drink
Pernod, Ricard

le vin
wine
*Champagne, Burgundy,
Muscadet*

la bière
beer
usually made in Alsace

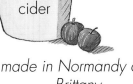

le cidre
cider

*made in Normandy and
Brittany*

l'eau minérale
mineral water
Perrier (bubbly), Evian (still)

la liqueur
after-dinner drink
Kirsch, Chartreuse

A French meal

Lunch **(le déjeuner)** and dinner **(le dîner)** are usually large meals and can go on for hours.

le repas
meal

The meal starts with soup or **hors d'oeuvres** (appetizers). Next there is a meat or fish course. The salad is often eaten after this.

The meal ends with cheese, followed by a dessert or fruit.

What people do

France is a large country, and people live and work differently in the various regions. Some people work in busy industrial areas. Others live in the countryside and are farmers.

France is an important farming country, but today machines do much of the work. Fewer people now work on the land than in industry.

Farmers grow cereals (wheat, oats, and barley), grapes, fruit, and vegetables. Dairy farmers produce cheese, butter, milk, cream, and yogurt.

le fermier
farmer

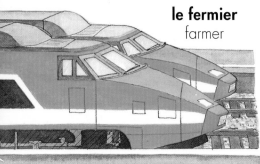

French railways employ many people. France's **Train à Grande Vitesse** (TGV) runs between towns all over the country and holds the world rail speed record.

Sheep farming is common in the southeast and the central plateau. Roquefort cheese is made from sheep's milk.

France is especially famous for its wine. The wine business employs many people, especially in the grape-picking season. The wines and brandies of France are sold all over the world.

le mouton
sheep

Steel, cars, shipbuilding, aircraft, textiles, perfume, and food products are some of France's main industries.

l'usine
factory

French farms and fisheries produce almost all the food the people need.

The people of Brittany (called Bretons) are mainly farmers and fishermen. Nearly half of the fish caught in the sea around France come from this region.

le pêcheur
fisherman

Figs, oranges, lemons, almonds, and olives are grown in the south, along the Mediterranean coast. Flowers are grown there, too, for making perfume. The perfume business is very important.

Many French people work in hotels and restaurants. There is an important tourist trade, especially in the Alps and along the Mediterranean coast.

17

Children in France

Here you can find out something about school life in France, and about how French children spend their time.

l'école
school

The school day usually begins at 8:30 in the morning and lasts until 4:00 in the afternoon. There may be classes on Saturday mornings, but Wednesdays are normally free.

les vacances
vacations

School children have several long vacations. They get: one week at **Toussaint** (All Saints) which is the autumn mid-term; two weeks at Christmas; two weeks at the end of February (winter mid-term); two weeks at Easter, and two months in the summer.

les devoirs
homework

At most French schools, children do not wear a uniform. Many of them wear jeans, a sweatshirt, and sneakers.

les vêtements
clothes

Though French children have long vacations, many of them have to do **devoirs de vacances** (vacation homework), reviewing what they have learned at school during the year.

Many schools also offer what they call **classe de neige** (class in the snow) or **classe de mer** (class by the sea). The whole class spends a week in a ski resort or at the seaside. Lessons go on as usual, but the children also do outdoor activities.

All children take part in sports at school.

le sport
sport

Athletics, gymnastics, and team sports such as football, volleyball, and basketball are played.

One of the favorite pastimes of many French children is reading comics. Characters such as Asterix and Tintin are very popular.

le skateboard
skateboarding

As in many other countries, there are crazes. Over recent years these have included skateboarding and electronic games

la bande dessinée
comics

History of France

58 B.C.

The Romans, led by Julius Caesar, invaded France (or Gaul, as it was then called). It remained part of the huge Roman Empire for 400 years.

1066

le roi
king

William the Conqueror (from Normandy, in northern France) invaded England, won the Battle of Hastings, and was crowned king of England.

1337–1453

During the Hundred Years War, England invaded France. The English won parts of France, but Joan of Arc inspired the French to rise up against them. She was captured by the English and burned to death in 1431. By 1453, the English had been defeated.

1789

In 1789, the French people decided to overthrow the king and nobles so the people themselves could rule the country. King Louis XVI, and many others, were beheaded. This was called the French Revolution.

le soldat
soldier

Liberty leading the people
– a painting by Delacroix

1830–1848

Napoleon Bonaparte was a brilliant soldier, who became the people's hero during the French Revolution. He crowned himself Emperor in 1804. He was defeated by the English at the Battle of Waterloo in 1815.

After the Battle of Waterloo, the French royal family and nobles tried to return to power. However, they were defeated by the people in two more revolutions in 1830 and 1848.

1919

During World War II (1939–1945), Hitler's troops invaded France. General Charles de Gaulle led the French Resistance fighters who worked to defeat the Germans. France was eventually freed in 1944.

1944

France lost the regions of Alsace and Lorraine to Germany during the Franco-Prussian War in 1870. However, at the Treaty of Versailles at the end of World War I (1914–1918), Germany gave them back to France.

1958

In 1958, France joined with West Germany, Italy, Belgium, the Netherlands, and Luxembourg to form the European Economic Community.

Famous places

Thousands of tourists from all over the world visit France every year. There are many beautiful and interesting places to see. Here are some of them.

Near Paris is the enormous and magnificent royal palace called the Château de Versailles, built 300 years ago for King Louis XIV.

le pique-nique
picnic

Visitors picnic beside the many lakes, fountains, and statues on the grounds.

Mont-Saint Michel was built as a monastery on a tiny island off the coast of Normandy. When the tide is low, you can walk or drive to it across the sand.

l'ile
island

Annecy is a beautiful old lakeside town in the Savoie region. Visitors like to go boating on the lake.

le lac
lake

le pont
bridge

The Pont du Gard is a huge aqueduct in Provence, built over 2,000 years ago by the Romans. It carried spring water 21 miles (35 km) into the town of Nimes.

The old town of Rouen in Normandy has an important place in French history. It was here that Joan of Arc was burned to death by the English for leading the French against them. A monument marks where she was burned.

Jeanne d'Arc
Joan of Arc

The Château de Chambord, in the Loire Valley, is one of France's most extravagant châteaux. It has 440 rooms and a maze of staircases and turrets.

Corsica, a lovely island in the Mediterranean Sea, is a popular place for vacations. You can enjoy deep-sea diving in the clear, warm water.

la plage
beach

Festivals

The French love celebrations. Many festivals are held throughout the year. Some celebrate religious occasions and historical events, others the arts. Some regions have their own festivals.

On July 14, everyone in France celebrates the storming of the Bastille prison at the beginning of the French Revolution. There are torchlit processions, military parades, and firework displays. People decorate their houses with flags and dance in the streets all night.

la fête
festival

le festival du film
film festival

There are many festivals celebrating the arts, including theater, cinema, dance, and music. The International Film Festival, held in Cannes every year, attracts famous stars and filmmakers who come to see the year's new films.

In some parts of northern France, huge models of local historical heroes, called **Les Géants** (the giants), are paraded through the streets during special festivals.

At Christmas, people ski down the mountains at night carrying flaming torches.

le géant
giant

In the big wine-producing areas, local people celebrate the end of the grape harvest every autumn.

They hold dances and taste the new wine. Members of the wine societies dress up in traditional costume.

le cyclisme
cycling

The Tour de France is a cycle race that is held each summer. Cyclists from all over the world take part. Millions watch the race, either along the route or on television.

l'âne
donkey

On December 6, people in the north and east celebrate the Festival of St. Nicholas (Father Christmas), the patron saint of children. In many towns a man dressed as St. Nicholas walks through the streets with a donkey, handing out sweets to children.

On January 6, the French celebrate **la Fête des Rois** (festival of the three kings). People eat a special cake, and whoever finds the bean hidden in it is King of the Day.

Mardi Gras is an enormous carnival held in Nice. For 12 days people watch the processions of colorful floats and people in fancy dress.

You can join in a battle of flowers with the people on floats.

le char
float

le cortège
procession

How to speak French

**Now you can find out how to speak French.
The Flaubert family show you what to say in many different
situations. Here they are to introduce themselves.**

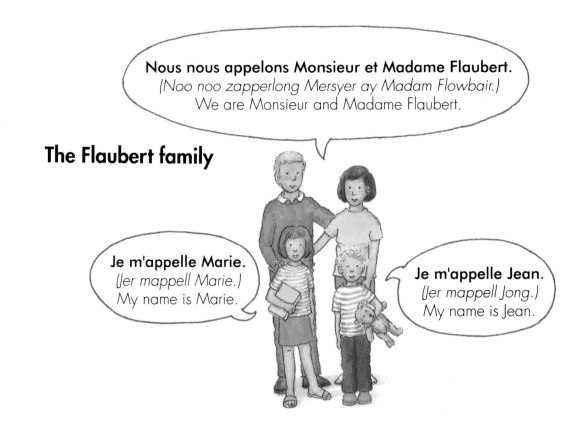

The Flaubert family

Nous nous appelons Monsieur et Madame Flaubert.
(Noo noo zapperlong Mersyer ay Madam Flowbair.)
We are Monsieur and Madame Flaubert.

Je m'appelle Marie.
(Jer mappell Marie.)
My name is Marie.

Je m'appelle Jean.
(Jer mappell Jong.)
My name is Jean.

**Everything the Flaubert family says is written in French
and English. There is also a guide to help you pronounce
the French words.**

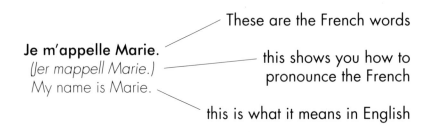

Je m'appelle Marie.
(Jer mappell Marie.)
My name is Marie.

These are the French words

this shows you how to
pronounce the French

this is what it means in English

How to say French words

The pronunciation guide shows you how to say the French words. These notes will help you to use the guide:

• When you see the letters 'ew', purse your lips as if you are going to make an 'oo' sound, but say 'ee' instead.

• When you see the letters 'er' in a pronunciation guide you should say them like the 'er' in under, but with a silent 'r'.

• You should say the letters 'ng' very quickly, so that the 'g' is almost silent. It should sound like the 'ng' of the word 'bang'.

• The letter 'j' is pronounced like the 's' in 'treasure'.

Accents

• French vowels often have marks called accents above them, such as **é**, **à** or **î**. Vowels with accents are pronounced differently from vowels without accents.

• The letter 'c' sometimes has an accent underneath it, eg in the word '**ç**a'. This letter 'c' should be pronounced like the 's' in 'sock', not like the 'c' in 'cat'.

Speaking to people

In French, there are two different words for 'you'. You use **tu** when you speak to a friend or an adult you know well. You use **vous** when you speak to more than one friend or an adult you do not know very well.

Masculine and feminine words

In French, some words are masculine and some are feminine. There are different words for 'the':

le salon   (masculine singular)
la porte   (feminine singular)

When the word begins with a vowel you use **l'**, eg **l'**église.

All plural words have the same word for 'the':

les salons (masculine plural)
les portes (feminine plural)

Meeting people

French people have different ways of greeting someone they meet. They use very polite greetings for people they do not know well and more friendly greetings for close friends.

Monsieur Flaubert meets a man he does not know very well.

> **Bonjour!**
> *(Bongjoor!)*
> Good morning!

> **Comment allez-vous?**
> *(Commong tallay-voo?)*
> How are you?

> **Bonjour, Monsieur Flaubert.**
> *(Bongjoor, Mersyer Flowbair.)*
> Good morning, Mr Flaubert.

> **Très bien, merci.**
> *(Tray beeyang, mairsee.)*
> Very well, thank you.

Marie and Jean meet their friends outside the shops.

> **Salut, ça va?**
> *(Salew, sah vah?)*
> Hello, how're you doing?

> **Ça va merci, et toi?**
> *(Sah vah mairsee, ay twah?)*
> Fine thank you, and you?

> **A bientôt.**
> *(Ah beeyangtoh.)*
> See you soon.

> **Au revoir.**
> *(Orvwahr.)*
> Goodbye.

Monsieur Flaubert welcomes visitors to his home for dinner.

Bonsoir!
(Bongswahr!)
Good evening!

The phrase 'Bonne nuit' is only used last thing at night.

Bonne nuit, maman.
(Bonn nwee, mamong.)
Good night, Mummy.

Bonne nuit, Jean.
(Bonn nwee, Jong.)
Good night, Jean.

When people meet, they often like to discuss the weather. You will find some phrases describing the weather on page 55.

'Bonjour' can also mean 'good afternoon' as well as 'good morning'.

BOUCHERIE

Bonjour, Madame. Il fait beau aujourd'hui, n'est-ce pas?
(Bongjoor, Madam. Eel fay boh ohjoordwee, nesspah?)
Good afternoon, madam. It's a fine day, isn't it?

Oui, il fait chaud.
(Wee, eel fay shoh.)
Yes, it is hot.

29

Making friends

The Flaubert family is at the beach for the day. Monsieur and Madame Flaubert are sunbathing with the rest of the family while Marie and Jean are busy making friends.

Marie and Edward introduce their brother and sister.

Voici mon frère Jean.
(Vwahsee mong frair Jong.)
This is my brother Jean.

Voici ma soeur Emily.
(Vwahsee mah serr Emily.)
This is my sister Emily.

Tu parles français?
(Tew pahrl frongssay?)
Do you speak French?

Pardon, je ne comprends pas.
(Pahrdong, jer ner comprong pah.)
Sorry, I do not understand.

The other members of the Flaubert family enjoy a restful afternoon.

la famille
(lah fammeeyer)
family

le père
(ler pair)
father

la grand-mère
(lah grong-mair)
grandmother

la mère
(lah mair)
mother

l'oncle
(longkler)
uncle

la tante
(lah tongt)
aunt

le grand-père
(ler grong-pair)
grandfather

Finding the way

Madame Flaubert and her children visit a town that they have not been to before.

Pardon Madame, y a t'il un café près d'ici?
(Pahrdong Madam, eeyateel ung kaffay pray deessee?)
Excuse me, is there a café near here?

Oui, Madame.
(Wee, Madam.)
Yes, madam.

C'est loin?
(Say lwang?)
Is it far?

C'est au coin de la rue.
(Say toh kwang der lah rew.)
It is on the corner of the street.

Merci.
(Mairsee.)
Thank you.

Je vous en prie.
(Jer voo zong pree.)
It is a pleasure.

Direction words

à gauche *(ah gohsh)* left	**derrière** *(derryair)* behind	**devant** *(dervong)* in front of	**à droite** *(ah drwaht)* right
à côté de *(ah kohtay der)* next to		**tout droit** *(too drwah)* straight on	**en face de** *(ong fass der)* opposite
jusqu'à *(jewsskah)* as far as	**près d'ici** *(pray deessee)* near here	**là-bas** *(lah-bah)* over there	**entre** *(ongtrer)* between

On their way to the station, Marie and Jean get lost.

Je me suis perdu.
(Jer mer swee pairdew.)
I am lost.

La gare est à droite.
(Lah garr ay tah drwaht.)
The station is on the right.

Où est la gare, s'il vous plaît?
(Oo ay lah garr, seelvooplay?)
Where is the station, please?

Places to ask for

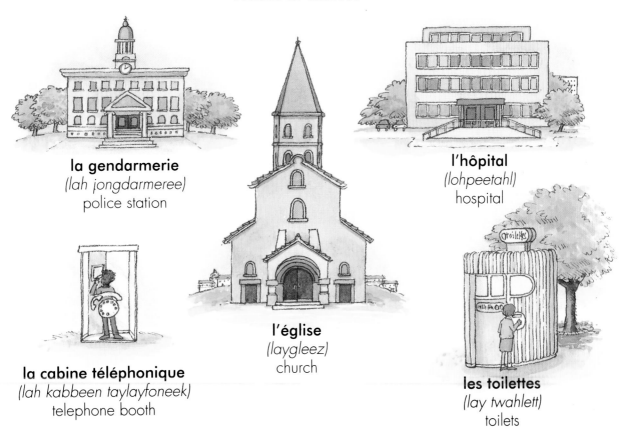

la gendarmerie
(lah jongdarmeree)
police station

l'hôpital
(lohpeetahl)
hospital

l'église
(laygleez)
church

la cabine téléphonique
(lah kabbeen taylayfoneek)
telephone booth

les toilettes
(lay twahlett)
toilets

Staying in a hotel or house

Monsieur and Madame Flaubert are on vacation at a hotel. While they are away, Marie and Jean stay at their grandparents' house.

Je voudrais réserver une chambre.
(Jer voodray rayzairvay ewn shongbrer.)
I would like to book a room.

Oui, Monsieur. Que désirez-vous?
(Wee, Mersyer. Ker dayzeeray-voo?)
Yes, sir. What would you like?

Une chambre pour deux personnes.
(Ewn shongbrer poor der pairsonn.)
A double room.

Le dîner est à quelle heure?
(Ler deenay ay tah kell err?)
What time is dinner?

A huit heures, Madame.
(Ah weet err, Madam.)
At eight o'clock, madam.

Voici votre clef, Monsieur.
(Vwahsee vottrer klay, Mersyer.)
Here is your key, sir.

le porteur
(ler porterr)
porter

la valise
(lah valeez)
suitcase

l'ascenseur
(lassongserr)
elevator

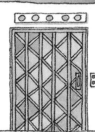
la clef
(lah klay)
key

le toit
(ler twah)
roof

la maison
(lah mayzong)
house

le grenier
(ler grernyay)
attic

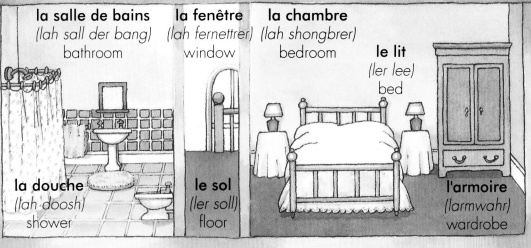

la salle de bains
(lah sall der bang)
bathroom

la fenêtre
(lah fernettrer)
window

la chambre
(lah shongbrer)
bedroom

le lit
(ler lee)
bed

la douche
(lah doosh)
shower

le sol
(ler soll)
floor

l'armoire
(larmwahr)
wardrobe

le fauteuil
(ler fohter-yer)
armchair

le salon
(ler sallong)
living room

la porte
(lah port)
door

la télévision
(lah taylayveezyong)
television

la cuisine
(lah kweezeen)
kitchen

la salle à manger
(lah sallamongjay)
dining room

la chaise
(lah shehz)
chair

la table
(lah tahbler)
table

l'escalier
(leskalyay)
staircase

Camping

le matelas pneumatique
(ler matterlah pnermatteek)
air mattress

le lit de camp
(ler lee der cong)
camp bed

l'eau
(loh)
water

le piquet
(ler peekay)
tent peg

Eau Potable

(Oh pohtahbler)
Drinking water

le réchaud
(ler rayshoh)
stove

It is the summer holidays. The Flaubert family is staying at a campsite that provides its own tents which are very comfortable.

Où est-ce que je peux prendre une douche?
(Oo essker jer per prongdrer ewn doosh?)
Where can I take a shower?

Là-bas, je crois.
(Lah-bah, jer crwah.)
Over there, I think.

(Rayzairvay oh caravan)
Recreational vehicles only

Réservé aux Caravanes

le tapis de sol
(ler tappee der soll)
groundsheet

la tente
(lah tongt)
tent

la caravane
(lah caravan)
camper

le maillet
(ler my-yay)
mallet

Je vais au magasin du camping.
(Jer vay zoh magazang dew congpeeng.)
I am going to the campsite shop.

Attends-moi!
(Attong-mwah!)
Wait for me!

le terrain de camping
(ler tairang der congpeeng)
campsite

TOILETTES
(Twahlett)
Toilets

la remorque
(lah rermork)
trailer

Parking Interdit
(Parkeeng angtairdee)
No parking

le camping gaz
(ler congpeeng gaz)
camping gas

le sac de couchage
(ler sack der cooshahj)
sleeping bag

Going shopping

The Flaubert family is out shopping. They visit the baker, the market and the newsstand.

The baker

Bonjour. Je voudrais deux pains, s'il vous plaît.
(Bongjoor. Jer voodray der pang, seelvooplay.)
Hello. I would like two loaves of bread, please.

Oui, bien sûr. C'est tout?
(Wee, beeyang sewr. Say too?)
Yes, certainly. Is that all?

Ça fait combien?
(Sah fay combeeyang?)
How much is that?

Ça fait sept francs cinquante, Madame.
(Sah fay sett frong sangkongt, Madam.)
That is seven francs fifty centimes, madam.

French money is divided into francs (F) and centimes (ct). There are 100 centimes in one franc. The numbers you will need to know for shopping are on page 55.

The market

Madame, vous désirez?
(Madam, voo dayzeeray?)
Can I help you, madam?

Un kilo de tomates, s'il vous plaît.
(Ung keeloh der tommaht, seelvooplay.)
A kilo of tomatoes, please.

les pommes
(lay pomm)
apples

les tomates
(lay tommaht)
tomatoes

The newsstand

Je voudrais un journal, s'il vous plaît.
(Jer voodray ung joornahl, seelvooplay.)
I would like a newspaper, please.

Combien coûtent les cartes postales?
(Combeeyang coot lay cart postahl?)
How much are the postcards?

Ça fait trois francs, Monsieur.
(Sah fay trwah frong, Mersyer.)
That is three francs, sir.

Deux francs la carte.
(Der frong lah cart.)
Two francs each.

Shopping words

faire des courses
(fair day coorss)
to go shopping

je voudrais
(jer voodray)
I would like

je regarde seulement
(jer rergard serlermong)
I am only looking

acheter
(ashtay)
to buy

coûter
(cootay)
to cost

un kilo
(ung keeloh)
a kilo

un litre
(ung leetrer)
a litre

ouvert
(oovair)
open

soldes
(solld)
sale

une livre
(ewn leevrer)
half a kilo

Combien coûte...?
(Combeeyang coot...?)
How much is...?

libre service
(leebrer sairveess)
self-service

les poires
(lay pwahr)
pears

les pommes de terre
(lay pomm der tair)
potatoes

les carottes
(lay carott)
carrots

les choux
(lay shoo)
cabbages

The post office and bank

Marie and Edward visit the post office while Madame Flaubert is at the bank.

Combien coûte un timbre pour une carte postale pour l'Angleterre?
(Combeeyang coot ung tangbrer poor ewn cart postahl poor long-glertair?)
How much is a stamp for a postcard to England?

Deux francs.
(Der frong.)
Two francs.

Je voudrais quatre timbres, s'il vous plaît.
(Jer voodray kahtrer tangbrer, seelvooplay.)
I would like four stamps, please.

Oui, bien sûr.
(Wee, beeyang sewr.)
Yes, certainly.

Où se trouve la boîte aux lettres?
(Oo ser troov lah bwahtt oh lettrer?)
Where is the mailbox?

Là-bas.
(Lah-bah.)
Over there.

POSTES

la lettre
(lah lettrer)
letter

le timbre
(ler tangbrer)
stamp

la télécopie
(lah taylaycoppee)
fax

la télécarte
(lah taylaycart)
telephone card

Pourriez-vous me donner de la monnaie?
(Pooreeay-voo mer donnay der lah monnay?)
Could I have some small change?

Puis-je changer un chèque de voyage ici?
(Pwee-jer shongjay ung sheck der vwah-yahj eessee?)
Can I cash a traveler's check here?

le billet
(ler beeyay)
bank note

la pièce
(lah pyess)
coin

le chèque de voyage
(ler sheck der vwah-yahj)
traveler's check

la monnaie
(lah monnay)
small change

Eating out

French people enjoy going out with friends and family for a drink or a meal.

Madame Flaubert meets a friend at a café.

The Flaubert family visits the countryside and enjoys a picnic in the sunshine.

It is Madame Flaubert's birthday. She and Monsieur Flaubert dine at a restaurant.

Useful words for eating out

Madame *(Madam)* waitress	**le menu** *(ler mernew)* menu	**la serviette** *(lah sairveeyett)* napkin	**l'addition** *(laddeessyong)* bill	**Monsieur** *(Mersyer)* waiter
la nappe *(lah napp)* tablecloth	**le couteau** *(ler kootoh)* knife	**la fourchette** *(lah foorshett)* fork	**la cuillère** *(lah kweeyair)* spoon	**le verre** *(ler vair)* glass

43

Visiting places

Monsieur and Madame Flaubert like to take their children to the movies and other places of entertainment.

Madame Flaubert takes Jean and Pierre to see a cartoon film.

J'adore les dessins animés.
(Jaddor lay dessang zannimay.)
I love cartoons.

Quel est le prix des places?
(Kell ay ler pree day plass?)
How much are the tickets?

CINEMA 1

ASTERIX

ASTERIX
14.30 –
16.00

Moi aussi.
(Mwah ohssee.)
Me too.

The Flaubert family often visits the tourist information center.
It has leaflets that show interesting places to visit.

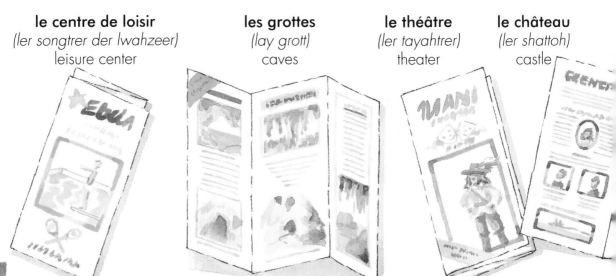

le centre de loisir
(ler songtrer der lwahzeer)
leisure center

les grottes
(lay grott)
caves

le théâtre
(ler tayahtrer)
theater

le château
(ler shattoh)
castle

The Flaubert family visits a sound and light show at a château. The show is called a 'son et lumière' *(sonnay lewmeeair)*. It tells the history of the château.

C'est très joli.
(Say tray jollee.)
It is very pretty.

Je suis fatigué.
(Jer swee fateegay.)
I am tired.

C'est intéressant, n'est-ce pas?
(Say tangtairessang, nesspah?)
It is interesting, isn't it?.

le cirque
(ler seerk)
circus

la réserve nationale
(lah raysairv nassyonal)
nature reserve

le musée
(ler mewzay)
museum

Games and sports

le rugby
(ler rergbee)
rugby

le golf
(ler golf)
golf

le football
(ler footbohll)
soccer

le ski
(ler skee)
skiing

la planche à voile
(lah plongsh ah vwahl)
windsurfing

l'aviron
(laveerong)
rowing

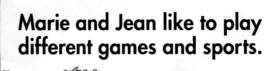

le ski nautique
(ler skee nohteek)
water skiing

Marie and Jean like to play different games and sports.

la balançoire
(lah ballongswahr)
swing

C'est à toi.
(Say tah twah.)
Your turn.

Est-ce que je peux jouer?
(Essker jer per jooay?)
Can I play?

les billes
(lay beeyer)
marbles

l'équitation
(laykitassyong)
riding

le patinage
(ler patteenahj)
skating

46

faire du jogging
(fair dew jogging)
to go jogging

le badminton
(ler badmeengtong)
badminton

la natation
(lah nahtassyong)
swimming

Attrape!
(Attrapp!)
Catch!

cache-cache
(cash-cash)
hide and seek

...Quatre, cinq, six...
(...Kahtrer, sangk, seess...)
...Four, five, six...

la pêche
(lah pesh)
fishing

le tennis
(ler tenneess)
tennis

les boules
(lay booll)
lawn bowling

la gymnastique
(lah jimnasteek)
gymnastics

le volleyball
(ler volleebohll)
volleyball

le cyclisme
(ler seekleezm)
cycling

Accidents and illnesses

In France, there are different telephone numbers for the police, the fire brigade and the ambulance service.

On m'a volé mon sac à main!
(Ong mah vollay mong sak ah mang!)
My handbag has been stolen.

Au feu!
(Oh fer!)
Fire!

Au secours!
(Oh sercoor!)
Help!

Venez vite!
(Vernay veet!)
Come quickly!

Accident words

l'agent de police
(lahjong der pohleess)
policeman

le pompier
(ler pongpyay)
fireman

l'ambulancier
(longbewlongssyay)
ambulance man

la voiture de police
(lah vwahtewr der pohleess)
police car

la voiture de pompiers
(lah vwahtewr der pongpyay)
fire engine

l'ambulance
(longbewlongss)
ambulance

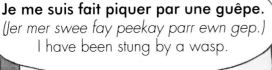

Je me suis fait piquer par une guêpe.
(Jer mer swee fay peekay parr ewn gep.)
I have been stung by a wasp.

J'ai attrapé un coup de soleil.
(Jay attrappay ung coo der sohlay.)
I am sunburnt.

l'aspirine
(laspeereen)
aspirin

le médecin
(ler medsang)
doctor

l'infirmière
(langfermeeair)
nurse

le pansement
(ler pongsmong)
self-adhesive bandage

J'ai mal à la tête.
(Jay mal ah lah tett.)
I have a headache.

Tu as de la fièvre.
(Tew ah der lah feeyairvrer.)
You have a temperature.

Je suis enrhumée.
(Jer swee zongrewmay.)
I have a cold.

J'ai mal au ventre.
(Jay mal oh vongtrer.)
I have a stomach ache.

Travelling

The Flaubert family travels by different kinds of transport.

Nous sommes en panne.
(Noo somm zong pann.)
We have broken down.

Où est le garage le plus proche?
(Oo ay ler garahj ler ploo prosh?)
Where is the nearest garage?

la voiture
(lah vwahtewr)
car

Un billet pour Paris.
(Ung beeyay poor Parree.)
A ticket to Paris.

Railway words

la gare
(lah garr)
station

la garde
(lah gard)
guard

l'horaire
(lorrair)
timetable

le quai
(ler kay)
platform

le guichet
(ler geeshay)
ticket office

le composteur
(ler congposterr)
ticket puncher

le bagage
(ler bagahj)
luggage

le billet
(ler beeyay)
ticket

la voiture-buffet
(lah vwahtewr-bewfay)
dining car

le chariot à bagages
(ler sharreeoh ah bagahj)
trolley

More useful words

Time

Quelle heure est-il, s'il te plaît?
(Kell err ayteel, seelterplay?)
What time is it?

Il est trois heures.
(Eel ay trwah zerr.)
It is three o'clock.

Il est trois heures dix.
(Eel ay trwah zerr deess.)
It is ten past three.

Il est trois heures et quart.
(Eel ay trwah zerr ay kahr.)
It is quarter past three.

Il est trois heures et demie.
(Eel ay trwah zerr ay dermee.)
It is half past three.

Il est quatre heures moins le quart.
(Eel ay kahtrer err mwang ler kahr.)
It is quarter to four.

Il est quatre heures moins dix.
(Eel ay kahtrer err mwang deess.)
It is ten minutes to four.

Il est midi.
(Eel ay meedee.)
It is midday.

Il est minuit.
(Eel ay meenwee.)
It is midnight.

Times of the day

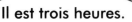

l'après-midi
(lappray-meedee)
afternoon

la nuit
(lah nwee)
night

le matin
(ler mattang)
morning

le soir
(ler swahr)
evening

The months of the year and days of the week

janvier
(jongveeay)
January

The French do not use capital letters at the beginning of words for months of the year or days of the week.

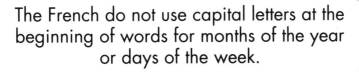

juillet
(jweeay)
July

février
(fayvreeay)
February

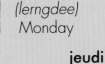

lundi *(lerngdee)* Monday	**mardi** *(mahrdee)* Tuesday	**mercredi** *(maircrerdee)* Wednesday
	jeudi *(jerdee)* Thursday	**vendredi** *(vongdrerdee)* Friday
	samedi *(sammdee)* Saturday	**dimanche** *(deemongsh)* Sunday

août
(oott)
August

mars
(mahrss)
March

The seasons

le printemps
(ler prangtong)
spring

l'été
(laytay)
summer

l'automne
(lohton)
autumn

l'hiver
(leevair)
winter

septembre
(sayptongbrer)
September

octobre
(oktohbrer)
October

novembre
(nohvongbrer)
November

avril
(avreel)
April

mai
(may)
May

juin
(jwang)
June

décembre
(dayssongbrer)
December

Clothes and parts of the body

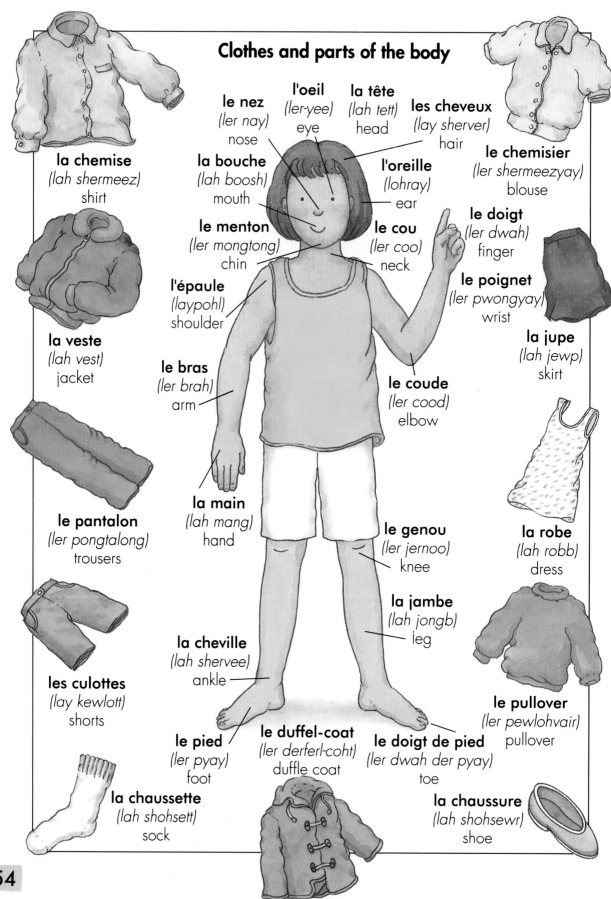

la chemise
(lah shermeez)
shirt

la veste
(lah vest)
jacket

le pantalon
(ler pongtalong)
trousers

les culottes
(lay kewlott)
shorts

la chaussette
(lah shohsett)
sock

le nez
(ler nay)
nose

l'oeil
(ler-yee)
eye

la tête
(lah tett)
head

les cheveux
(lay sherver)
hair

le chemisier
(ler shermeezyay)
blouse

la bouche
(lah boosh)
mouth

l'oreille
(lohray)
ear

le doigt
(ler dwah)
finger

le menton
(ler mongtong)
chin

le cou
(ler coo)
neck

le poignet
(ler pwongyay)
wrist

l'épaule
(laypohl)
shoulder

la jupe
(lah jewp)
skirt

le bras
(ler brah)
arm

le coude
(ler cood)
elbow

la main
(lah mang)
hand

le genou
(ler jernoo)
knee

la robe
(lah robb)
dress

la jambe
(lah jongb)
leg

la cheville
(lah shervee)
ankle

le pied
(ler pyay)
foot

le duffel-coat
(ler derferl-coht)
duffle coat

le doigt de pied
(ler dwah der pyay)
toe

le pullover
(ler pewlohvair)
pullover

la chaussure
(lah shohsewr)
shoe

54

Colours and numbers

1 un *(ung)*

2 deux *(der)*

3 trois *(trwah)*

4 quatre *(kahtrer)*

5 cinq *(sangk)*

6 six *(seess)*

7 sept *(sett)*

8 huit *(weet)*

9 neuf *(nerf)*

10 dix *(deess)*

11 onze *(ongz)*

12 douze *(dooz)*

13 treize *(trayz)*

14 quatorze *(kattorz)*

15 quinze *(kangz)*

16 seize *(sayz)*

17 dix-sept *(dee-sett)*

18 dix-huit *(dee-zweet)*

19 dix-neuf *(dee-znerf)*

jaune *(johne)* yellow

orange *(orongj)* orange

rouge *(rooj)* red

vert *(vair)* green

bleu *(bler)* blue

blanc *(blong)* white

noir *(nwahr)* black

rose *(roze)* pink

gris *(gree)* gray

brun *(brerng)* brown

The weather

Il fait beau.
(Eel fay boh.)
It is fine.

Il fait froid.
(Eel fay frwah.)
It is cold.

Il fait du soleil.
(Eel fay dew sohlay.)
It is sunny.

Il pleut.
(Eel pler.)
It is raining.

Il fait chaud.
(Eel fay shoh.)
It is hot.

Il fait du vent.
(Eel fay dew vong.)
It is windy.

20 vingt *(vang)*

21 vingt et un *(vang tay ung)*

22 vingt-deux *(vang-der)*

30 trente *(trongt)*

40 quarante *(karrongt)*

50 cinquante *(sangkongt)*

60 soixante-dix *(swassongt-deess)*

70 soixante *(swassongt)*

80 quatre-vingts *(kahtrer-vang)*

90 quatre-vingt-dix *(kahtrer-vang-deess)*

100 cent *(song)*

1,000 mille *(meel)*

1,000,000 million *(meelyong)*

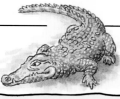

le crocodile
(ler crocohdeel)
crocodile

Index

la baleine
(lah bahlenn)
whale

l'ours
(loorss)
bear

le loup
(ler loo)
wolf

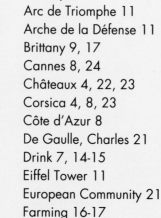

le panda
(ler pongda)
panda

le tigre
(ler teegrer)
tiger

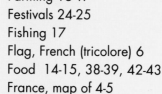

le dauphin
(ler dohfang)
dolphin

le zèbre
(ler zebrer)
zebra

le gorille
(ler goreeyer)
gorilla

le lion
(ler leeong)
lion

le kangourou
(ler kongooroo)
kangaroo

l'éléphant
(laylayfong)
elephant

la girafe
(lah jeeraff)
giraffe